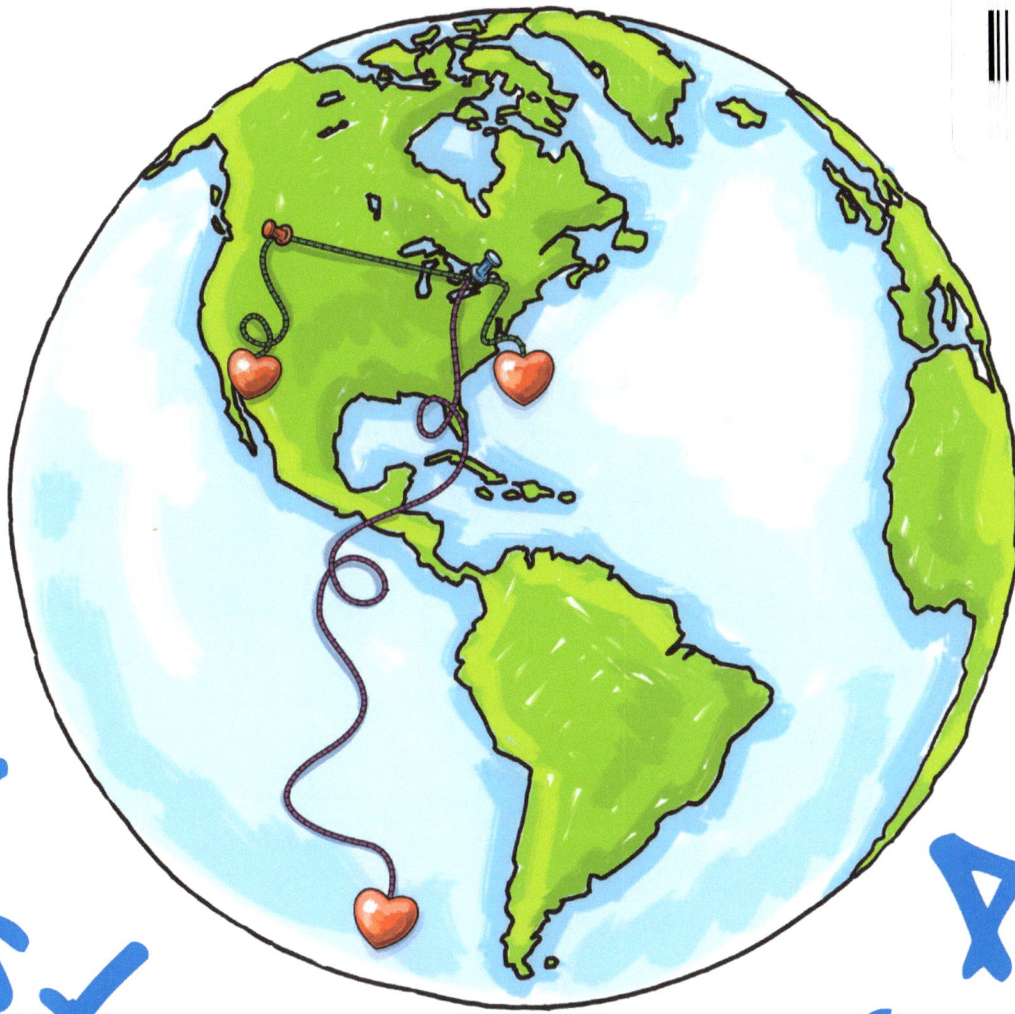

Just a String Away

Written by Sonya Anderson
Illustrated by Jon Larter

Written by Sonya Anderson
Illustrated by Jon Larter

ISBN 978-0-9939509-0-2

Published by Sizzle and Sim Productions
620 Veterans Drive Unit #2, Suite 21
Barrie, Ontario
L4N 9J4

www.SizzleAndSim.com

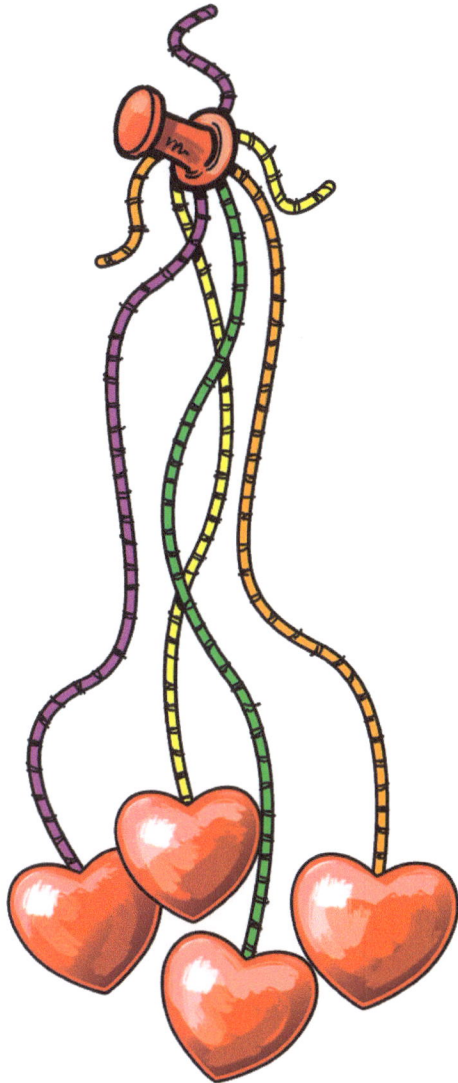

For my boys, Lyndon, Connor, and Jack, who are the inspiration for my stories.

For my mom, who instilled in me a love of reading and taught me the importance of reading with expression.

Special thanks to my sisters for their help editing.

And to Andrea R.G. who made me realize that a story worth telling was a story worth writing.

Once upon a map . . . there were two young brothers who loved sharing story time together. Big brother, Connor, had just finished reading a story to his little brother, Jack, when Jack sighed, "I miss Dad. Why does he have to go away so much?"

"Silly," Connor replied, "Dad's a pilot, he flies all over the world. That's his job."

"I know," Jack said, "but I miss him when he's gone."

"I know what you need," Connor said with a smile, "I'll be right back."

Jack watched with great curiosity as Connor sorted through his closet and raced around the house, gathering a few simple supplies. Soon Connor came back with a map, some string, and a handful of tacks.

"I've got a secret to share with you," Connor said with a grin. "It's a secret Mom told me a long time ago, even before you were born."

Connor took the map and hung it on the wall beside Jack's rocking chair. Then he put several tacks on the map and tied pieces of string to the tacks.

"See the red tack? That's Calgary, that's where we used to live. That's where Grandma and Grandpa still live. This blue tack is where we live now and this green string is the string that joins us together," Connor explained.

"Years ago when we moved from Calgary to Toronto it made me feel sad to leave our family and friends behind. Mom gave me this map and string and shared this secret with me that I am now sharing with you. **'No matter how far apart we may seem we are really just a string away'.**"

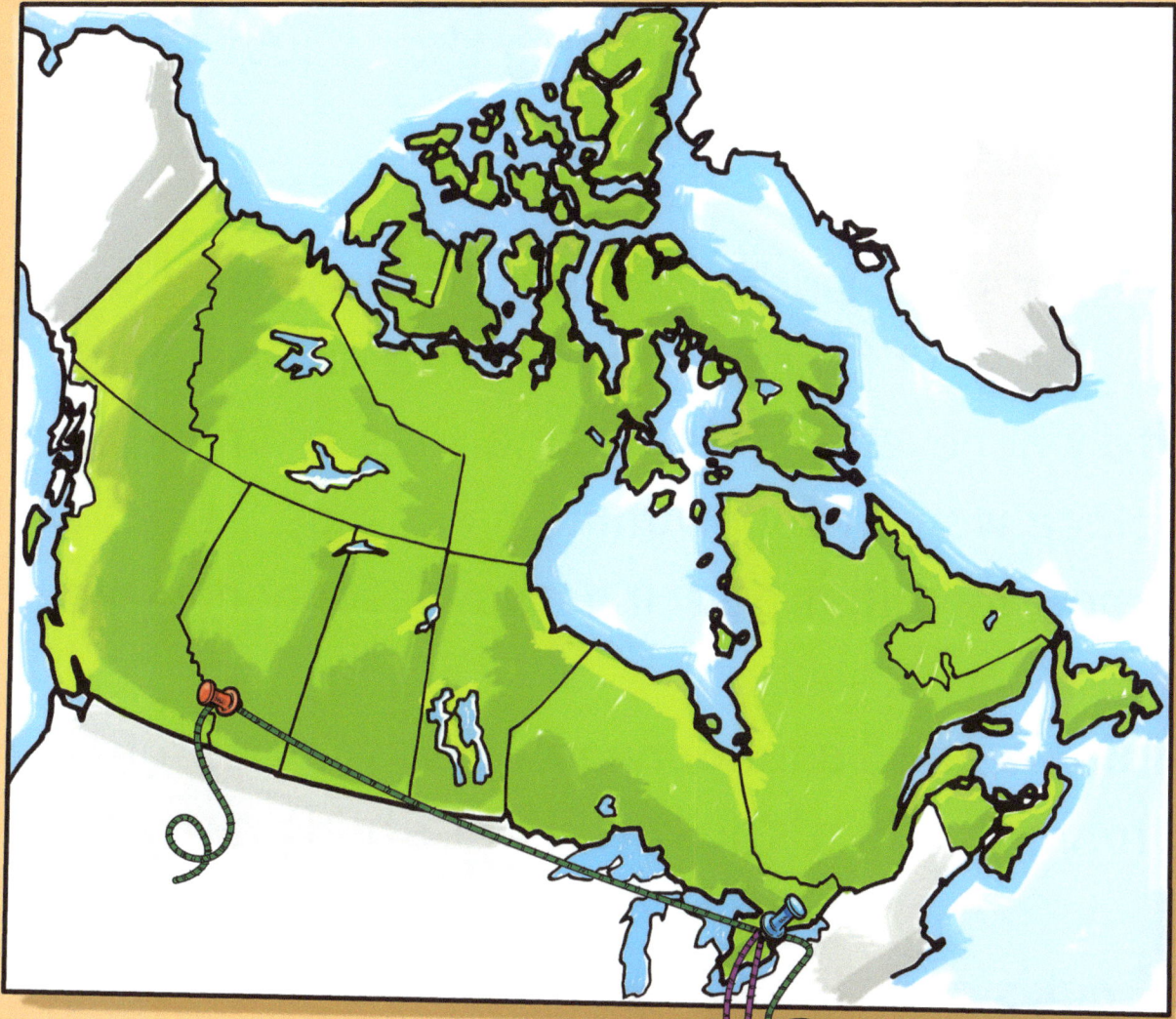

"What's this purple string that's just dangling here for?" Jack wondered.

"That's the **Daddy String**," Connor said with a grin. "It starts at our house and reaches to wherever Dad is. As he flies from place to place we can follow him on our map. Then we know **he's** just a string away," Connor explained.

"Come see," said Connor, "Dad's in Boston tonight. That's just a short string away."

Jack's eyes lit up. He still missed his Dad but it made him feel good to know he was so close.

That night when the boys called their Dad at his hotel, Jack quickly gushed, "You're in Boston, Dad, that's just a short string away!"

Connor and Mom looked at each other and shared a knowing wink. Connor was pleased that his little secret made his brother feel so good, and Mom was proud that Connor had shared the secret with his younger brother.

Over the years Connor and Jack shared countless stories together in that rocking chair. And they found it fascinating to track with their map and string all of the wonderful places that their Dad flew to.

They were also growing up and starting to dream big dreams about what they wanted to be when they grew up. Connor wanted to be an astronaut who travelled to the moon and explored its rocky surface. Jack wanted to be a firefighter who slid down fire poles, drove a noisy fire truck, and rescued people who needed help.

Mom listened to their dreams with a smile, although she couldn't help but think about how much she would miss her two boys when they were all grown up.

Then, one day, she found a special surprise waiting for her in her bedroom.

Connor — with help from Jack — had hung up two maps on the wall. One was a City map with a tack on their house, a tack on the fire hall, and a string in between linking the two.

The other was a map of the Solar System with a tack on Earth, a tack on the Moon, and a string joining them. This map also had a dangling string hanging from the tack on Earth. It could stretch as far as the farthest planet in our Solar System.

With a gleam in their eyes and a hug for their Mom, Connor and Jack said, "You never know just how far we may go Mom, but we'll both always be just a string away!"

Note to Grownups

You too can provide comfort to your loved one during a difficult time: a family separation, a move to a new city, military deployment, or to ease the anxiety of a child whose parent must travel for their work.

All it takes is some string, a few tacks, and a map scaled to the size that you will need. The map can be as big as the Solar System, or as small as a City map that can show that one family member lives or works on the other side of town!

When your children are involved in this activity, you'll be amazed at how much more effectively they are able to cope with separation from their loved one — and they'll learn a thing or two about geography in the process!

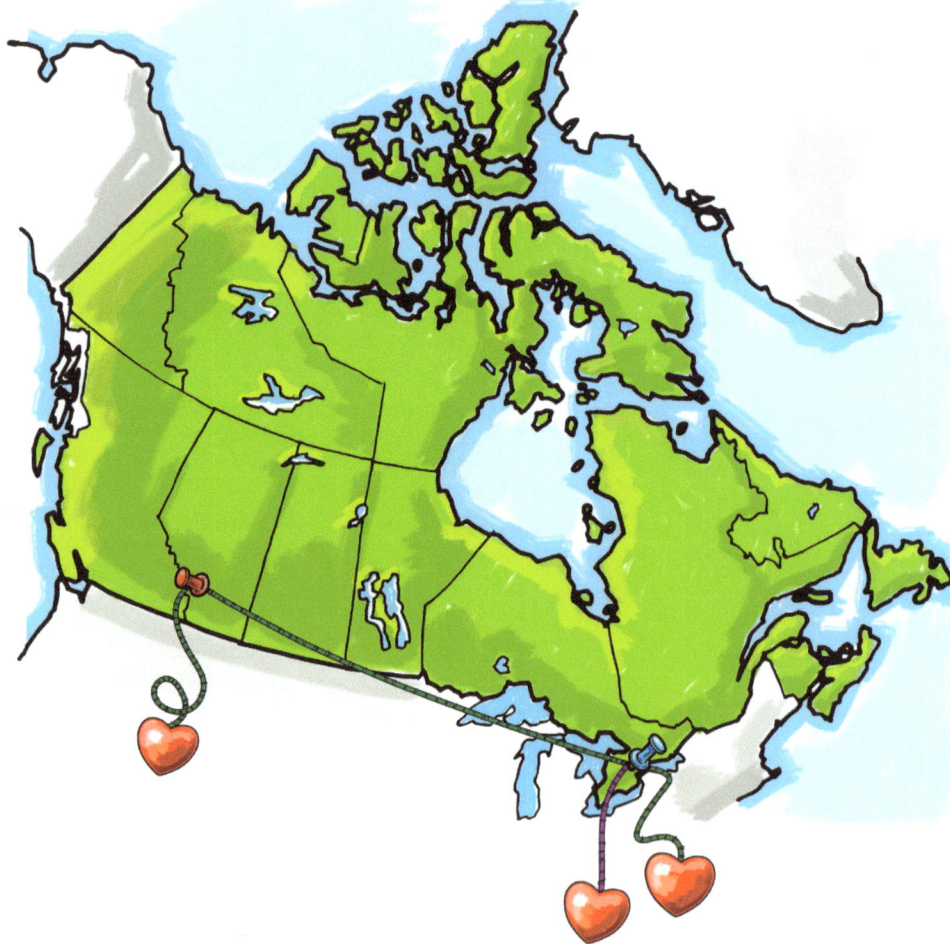

"Miles apart, but still in my heart... and always just a String Away!"

Visit www.SizzleAndSim.com for other books and products by Sonya Anderson.

www.ingramcontent.com/pod-product-compliance
Lightning Source LLC
Chambersburg PA
CBHW040024050426
42452CB00002B/120